Shame & Guilt

p 25 A major source of anxiety is the effort to will what cannot be willed

Hindsfoot Foundation Series
on Treatment and Recovery

Shame & Guilt

Ernest Kurtz

Second edition,
revised and updated

iUniverse, Inc.
New York Lincoln Shanghai

Shame & Guilt

iUniverse books may be ordered through booksellers or by contacting:

iUniverse
2021 Pine Lake Road, Suite 100
Lincoln, NE 68512
www.iuniverse.com
1-800-Authors (1-800-288-4677)

Because of the dynamic nature of the Internet, any Web addresses or links contained in this book may have changed since publication and may no longer be valid.

Second edition, revised and updated.
Originally published as *Shame and Guilt: Characteristics of the Dependency Cycle (A Historical Perspective for Professionals)*, Hazelden, 1981.

ISBN: 978-0-595-45492-1 (pbk)
ISBN: 978-0-595-89802-2 (ebk)

Printed in the United States of America

Contents

PART IV: Conclusion

Prefatory Note

This work—these ideas—were first presented in a booklet aimed primarily at alcoholism counselors and people in recovery from alcoholism. Much of the presentation in this updated revision remains couched in that language: whatever wisdom appears here necessarily derives most directly from the experience, strength, and hope of members of Alcoholics Anonymous and offspring Twelve-Step fellowships and programs.

But over the years I have discovered that these ideas have a far wider application. For in a very real sense, *alcoholic* is but "human being" writ large. Alcoholics are human beings who are both more and less than "merely human." And so, if you will pardon the momentary grandiosity, the audience for this book is humanity.

Which is one reason why it is being made available once again via this updated Hindsfoot Foundation edition.

A final introductory note: although the origin of this booklet's first edition meant that it sometimes dipped into the vocabulary of therapy, I have attempted in this revision to translate its ideas into the "language of the heart" that invites identification by all.

Introduction

✦

A Lesson from Alcoholics Anonymous

Two distinct ways of feeling "bad" afflict every human being. How those afflictions work—and how they can be healed—find clearest expression in the lives of alcoholics and addicts.[a] Neither experience is unique to the alcoholic, but each has a special place in the process of recovery from alcoholism. In this area perhaps more than in any other, alcoholism and its healing contribute to our knowledge of the human condition. They do this first by revealing the importance of distinguishing between these two often-confused phenomena. Most hurting people could profit from learning this distinction, but for alcoholics and addicts, learning and living it become a matter of life and death. The distinction is between **guilt** and **shame**.

[a] Throughout the text, although in general only the terms "alcohol," "alcoholic," and "alcoholism" will be used, the concept of addiction intends to include all mood-altering substances, all substance-dependent people, and all forms of substance dependency.

Shame differs from guilt. Because they differ, any effective healing of their diverse ways of "feeling bad" must differ. Some modes of healing, for some conditions, can afford to ignore the distinction between guilt and shame. But such is not the case with the alcoholic or with many other sufferers. Most hurting persons, and certainly the alcoholic, suffer *both* guilt and shame. And for the alcoholic, distinguishing between guilt and shame and confronting *each* constructively is necessary not only to attain sobriety but—perhaps more importantly—to maintain ongoing recovery, to attain a life that is genuinely "happy, joyous, and free."

Sobriety, the experience of Alcoholics Anonymous teaches, has two phases: first it must be attained; then it must be maintained. Attaining and maintaining—getting and keeping—sobriety require different but related emphases.[b] As Bill Wilson (quoting Doctor Bob Smith) told one group of alcoholism professionals: "Honesty gets us sober, but tolerance keeps us sober."[1] The honesty that lies at the heart of the A.A. program forces the distinction between guilt and shame. The tolerance that infuses the A.A. fellowship fosters continuing constructive confrontation with both.

> [b]"Sobriety" has been understood and presented, over the years, as synonymous with *serenity*, even with *sanctity*. In what follows, the reader is encouraged to use and think in whatever term best fits her or his condition: the effort of any of these terms is to name that condition of living that is, in the words of the book *Alcoholics Anonymous*, "happy, joyous, and free."

Confronting guilt, though painful, is not difficult. The beginner in Alcoholics Anonymous finds guilt allayed, indeed, by the very concepts of powerlessness and unmanageability that invite him to confront also his shame. The recovering alcoholic finds further help in dealing with guilt in the inventory and amendment Steps (Four, Five, Eight, and Nine) of the A.A. program, which guide directly to guilt's resolution.

The Twelve Steps of
Alcoholics Anonymous

1. We admitted we were powerless over alcohol—that our lives had become unmanageable.

2. Came to believe that a Power greater than ourselves could restore us to sanity.

3. Made a decision to turn our will and our lives over to the care of God *as we understood Him*.

4. Made a searching and fearless moral inventory of ourselves.

5. Admitted to God, to ourselves, and to another human being the exact nature of our wrongs.

6. Were entirely ready to have God remove all these defects of character.

7. Humbly asked Him to remove our shortcomings.

8. Made a list of all persons we had harmed, and became willing to make amends to them all.

9. Made direct amends to such people wherever possible, except when to do so would injure them or others.

10. Continued to take personal inventory and when we were wrong promptly admitted it.

11. Sought through prayer and meditation to improve our conscious contact with God *as we understood Him*, praying only for knowledge of His will for us and the power to carry that out.

12. Having had a spiritual awakening as the result of these steps, we tried to carry this message to alcoholics, and to practice these principles in all our affairs.

The confrontation with shame, although also set in motion by A.A.'s First Step, proves more tricky—and, for most, more difficult. Again, the A.A. program—all of it, but especially Steps Two, Six, Seven, and Ten—suggests shame's solution. It is Alcoholics Anonymous as fellowship that makes real this solution, but it is only in the conjunction with the Twelve Steps as program that the full benefits of A.A as fellowship can be real-ized—*made real.*

The impressive success of Alcoholics Anonymous in dealing with alcoholism and addiction flows directly from A.A.'s effectiveness at healing shame.[c]

[c]This is also why so many other therapies for difficulties far removed from alcoholism—obesity, grief, certain deforming diseases, for example—build their programs on A.A.'s Twelve Steps. The whole "Self-

Help Mutual Aid Group Movement" owes its philosophy and most of its modalities to Alcoholics Anonymous.[2]

Other therapies fail, especially over time, because un-faced shame proves much more dangerous to the alcoholic, especially in recovery, than does unresolved guilt. An appreciation of Alcoholics Anonymous as specifically a modality for the healing of shame thus can offer much ... and not only to the alcoholic.

PART I

Discovering and Recognizing Shame

1

Definitions: Embarrassment, Guilt, and Shame

Because of the general confusion about guilt and shame, both terms periodically tend to fall into disuse. "Guilt" thus seems mainly a legal concept, while the word "shame" is reserved for training children and animals. The reasons behind this confusion are complex. In briefest outline, modern psychology's distinctions between "rational" and "irrational" guilt, between "true guilt" and "guilty fear," have combined with a psychological age's mistrust of moralism to render most people suspicious of and uncomfortable with the word "guilt" except in contexts narrowly psychiatric or legal. "Shame" suffers from its association with upbringing and helpless dependency: it carries connotations of being "caught" and the implication that a consistently mature person will have no occasion to feel such disgrace.

But that very implication invites probing deeper. "Shame" is tricky, even treacherous: its usual understanding contains a trap. As commonly thought of, "shame" seems a virtual synonym for "embarrassment"; that is, to result from being seen by another. This misunderstanding arises, perhaps, because as children we learn the meaning of "shame" when someone projects it upon us. "You should be ashamed of yourself" is a reproach of public behavior—of something one is seen or caught doing. But the essence of shame consists not in being seen or being caught, but in *what* about one is seen, in *what* one is caught doing. "Embarrassment," then, is not a synonym for shame, but the result of one's shame being seen. "Being seen" or "being caught" are not the essence of shame: we are all seen by others, often and diversely. At times, indeed, we relish being seen: our

3

moments of success and triumph are enhanced by having an audience. "Being seen," then, is not the core even of embarrassment. The heart of embarrassment is that another sees our shame. The sense of shame comes before the sense of being seen—before, then, any advertence to "other."

Shame inheres in us, in ourselves—indeed, literally in our *self*. "Others," as we shall explore, are neither the problem in nor the source of shame; rather, others offer the only solution for shame. This is why it is so important to distinguish clearly between the "embarrassment" of being seen by others and the *shame* that comes in the recognition of the reality of our own self.

Both guilt and shame involve feeling "bad"—feeling bad about one's actions (or omissions) in the case of guilt; feeling bad about one's self in shame. What does it mean to *feel bad*? The deepest meaning of the word *bad* is "unable to fit": unable to fit into some external context in the case of guilt, unable to fit into one's own being in the case of shame. For there are, in human experience, two different ways of discovering that one does not "fit," of feeling "bad." Each has to do with the boundaries of the human condition.

An image may help to clarify the distinction and its point.

To be human is to be surrounded by boundaries: it is somewhat like standing in the middle of a football field during a game. As on a football field, there are two kinds of boundaries: side-lines and end-lines. The side-lines are containing *boundaries*: to cross them is to "go out of bounds," to do something wrong. The end-lines are *goal*-lines: the purpose of the game is to cross them. One feels "bad" (guilty) when one crosses the side-line, the restraining boundary. Feeling "bad" about the goal-line (shame) arises not from crossing it but from *not* crossing it, from failing to attain it.

Guilt, in this image, arises from the violation—transgression, stepping across—of some limiting boundary; shame occurs when a goal—an end—is not reached, is fallen short of. Guilt thus indicates an infraction, a breaking of the rules; shame, a literal "shortcoming," a lack or defect of being. The following schema may clarify:

	GUILT	SHAME
Results from:	A violation, a transgression, a fault of **doing**; the exercise of power or control.	A failure, a falling short, a fault of **being**, the failure of power or control.
Concerned with:	A separate, discrete act, some law or rule; one is guilty **for** something.	The overall **self**; some ideal or principle; one is ashamed **of** self.
Results in:	Feeling of wrong-doing; sense of wickedness; "**not** good"; fear of punishment.	Feeling of inadequacy; sense of worthlessness; "**no** good"; "not good **enough**"; fear of abandonment.
"Feels like":	Pang.	Ache.
Repair by:	Opposite acts, "making amends"; can be quantified.	As qualitative rather than quantitative, requires: new way of seeing (insight), change in **be**-ing (conversion).
	Reformed	Transformed
Possible outcome:	Surmounting guilt can lead to feelings of righteousness.	Transcending shame opens to a sense of identity and of freedom-as-human.
In psychoanalytic vocabulary:	Has to do with superego.	Has to do with ego ideal.

This understanding of guilt and shame suggests four topics for investigation:

(1) how to distinguish between guilt and shame in actual human experience;

(2) the significance of this distinction for understanding the human condition;

(3) the specific qualities of shame that enable its identification; and

(4) the nature of healing for shame.

We shall examine each topic in turn, keeping always in mind that our effort aims to derive effective insight from the actual experience of Alcoholics Anonymous.

Distinguishing between guilt and shame

The first difficulty to be confronted arises from the fact that guilt and shame usually come mingled, together. Although they are distinct experiences, guilt and shame rarely present themselves separately. Most transgressions, violations of some rule, also involve a failure, falling short of some ideal. If I steal, I not only violate someone else's right; I also fall short of my ideal of honesty. The same act (or omission) can thus give rise to *both* guilt and shame: one can experience shame and guilt over the same thing.

The success of Alcoholics Anonymous testifies that in such cases of mingled guilt and shame experienced after a transgression that is also a falling short, distinguishing between guilt and shame and treating first the shame are essential conditions of therapeutic effectiveness. Let us examine, then, how and why.

Distinguishing between guilt and shame is not difficult: it can be heard in the *accent* informing self-blame, in the dual emphasis that inheres in any description of feeling "bad."

Guilt focuses on the *thing done* and thus reveals itself in self-reproaches that run: how could I have *done* that; what an injurious *thing* to have done; how I hurt *so-and-so*; what a moral lapse that *act* was!

Simultaneously, however, shame attends to *self as do-er*, inducing self-reproaches with a very different emphasis: how could *I* have done that; what an idiot *I* am; what a *fool*; how awful and worthless *I* am![3]

Those who would attempt to heal, to make whole, persons harboring such mixed feelings—the mixture revealed by the differing accents in "What have I *done*?" and "What have *I* done?"—must be sensitive to both components. Too often, therapists settle for the resolution of guilt when it is the confrontation with shame that is the hurting person's deepest need. Indeed, a superficial reading of the A.A. Steps—one that sees the 4th, 5th, 8th, and 9th Steps in isolation from the rest of the Alcoholics Anonymous program—can reinforce this too often tragic error. Those Steps do deal effectively with guilt, but they are only part of the A.A. program. They come embedded, that is to say, in a life-shaping experience oriented primarily to the confrontation with shame.

What is this confrontation with shame and how is it achieved? The encounter involves finding, in experiences of shame, truth about the reality of human existence. It means learning, from experiences of falling short, wisdom concerning the meaning of being human. Shame, as its accenting reveals, focuses on the *self*: it is the perception of not just any lack or failure, but of the deficiency of the self as self, as human being. Shame testifies not to wrong-doing but to flawed be-ing.

Perhaps surprisingly, despite the depth of self involved in shame's feeling "bad," the sense of shame itself is a good thing—something to be cherished and valued. If this claim that shame is "good" seems strange, reflect for a moment on shame's opposite: indeed, think about the opposites of both guilt and shame. "Guiltless" is clearly a term of praise: to be guiltless, free from guilt, is to be innocent, blameless. "Shameless," on the other hand, is an epithet of condemnation and opprobrium. To be shameless is to be insensible to oneself, insensitive to one's self. One who lacks shame is impudent, brazen, without decency.[4]

Shame, then, despite its negative side that points up failure and falling short, also entails something positive: insight into the reality of the human condition. The experience of shame highlights the essential existential paradox that inheres in be-ing human: to be human is to be caught in a contradictory tension between the pull to the unlimited, the more-than-human, and the drag of the merely limited, the less-than-human. There are two difficult concepts here—essential limitation and the human as "middle." We shall examine each of them in turn, carefully, in the light shed by the experience of Alcoholics Anonymous.

2

The Experience and Acceptance of Essential Limitations

Step 1

Alcoholics Anonymous teaches as fundamental first truth the ultimate reality of personal essential limitation. "We admitted that we were powerless over alcohol—that our lives had become unmanageable." A.A. addresses itself not to the thing, alcoholism, but to the person, the alcoholic; and the First Step of its program states clearly, simply, and thoroughly that the alcoholic is essentially limited. "Powerless . . unmanageable": the acknowledgment "I am an alcoholic" that is inherent in these admissions accepts as first truth personal essential limitation. The newcomer to Alcoholics Anonymous is thus led to admit, to accept, and to embrace fundamental finitude—essential limitation—as the definition of her alcoholic human condition.

The concept of "*essential* limitation" comes hard: if it poses problems for philosophers, how can it be learned by the lowly alcoholic—indeed, not only learned but inculcated into the very marrow of his being? The program and fellowship of Alcoholics Anonymous accomplish this in several ways, ways that we shall explore in unfolding detail. Here, we focus on the first two: the idea of "alcoholic" and the significance of "the first drink."

The two are related. The "alcoholic," A.A. teaches, is one who cannot drink *any* alcohol safely. There is an essential "not"—an inherent limitation—in the very concept of "alcoholic." This "not" is an essential rather than an accidental limitation, because it applies to the first drink. We all know the gropings of the active alcoholic who realizes that he is in trouble—his staunch efforts to stop drinking before drunkenness, his tortured attempts to determine what is "his limit": two drinks? four beers? only with meals? A.A., in teaching that "the first drink gets the alcoholic drunk," inculcates that the alcoholic does not "have a limit": she *is* limited—and this is the meaning of essential limitation.

To be confronted by one's own essential limitation, to perceive oneself as essentially limited: these are narrowing, choking, tightening experiences. We experience these sensations in our innards, and we struggle against their implications with all our might. But struggle and might aggravate rather alleviate the pain. Although anyone who has felt that pain can never forget it, the sensation is difficult to name. Philosophers have called it *Angst* or *angoisse*; in English, the dreads of "anxiety" and "anguish." All of these terms drive from the same ancient source: ANGH, a primitive root the very sound of which conveys the sense of choked tightness gasped when something squeezes around one's throat. Although difficult to name, this sense is all too familiar to the alcoholic struggling with his addiction—the clutching feeling of dread that arises from the recognition that one is out of control. ANGH is the rub of finitude, reminding of essential limitation.[5]

Alcoholism is an experience of ANGH: it brings home the realization that to be human is to be essentially limited. The first response to this reminder is shame. The pain of ANGH arises, indeed, because something else within "being human" strives to reach beyond limitation and seeks to impose that one is not limited—insists, in short, that any limitation marks the failure of falling short. Here, on the field of essential limitation, Alcoholics Anonymous first wrestles with the alcoholic's shame.

The lesson is unwelcome and difficult; and therefore Alcoholics Anonymous teaches in several ways this insight that, because the first truth for the alcoholic is essential limitation, the first act required for the alcoholic to begin recovery is the acceptance of essential limitation. Most striking, perhaps, because so often misunderstood, is how A.A. inculcates this truth by applying the insight to itself.

At its very birth, Alcoholics Anonymous departed Oxford Group auspices because the Group, with its heritage of Christian perfectionism as revealed in its emphasis upon "The Four Absolutes," seemed both to demand and to claim too much. Because of this intuition that—at least for alcoholics—the problem of the Oxford Group, as well as one off-putting aspect of all organized religion, was that they claimed to do too much, Alcoholics Anonymous focused attention on its own limitations. Thus, A.A.'s claim that its fellowship and program are "spiritual rather than religious" involves not so much a rejection of religion as a profession of the acceptance of limitation. This understanding is confirmed by another Alcoholics Anonymous axiom, one especially dear to the heart and pen of its only philosopher, William Griffith Wilson. Bill made the point consistently, in many private letters as well as in his published writings, that even as "spiritual," A.A. was but "a kindergarten of the spirit."[6] He intended the image both to ensure A.A.'s own humility, its acceptance of its very real limitations, and to encourage A.A. members to grow in sobriety—and spirituality—in their own individual ways.

The fact of fundamental finitude and the need to accept this essential limitation pervade the fellowship and program of Alcoholics Anonymous. They are clear in the oft-repeated A.A. mottoes, "First Things First" and "One Day at a Time." The emphasis upon accepting limitation infuses A.A.'s own description of "How It Works" from the "Rarely" that opens that key fifth chapter of its Big Book, through the "tried to" that lies at the heart of its Twelfth Step, to its concluding qualification of its promise of "progress rather than ... perfection."[7]

Honesty concerning essential limitation is therefore the core of Alcoholics Anonymous. Such honesty thus becomes both the price and the reward, both the process and the purpose, of the A.A. member's First Step acceptance of himself as "powerless over alcohol." In a way suggestive of the psychoanalytic contract, Alcoholics Anonymous has intuited the existential truth that accepting the reality of self-as-feared is the essential precondition of finding the reality of self-as-is.

between animal & angel — all humans essentially limited

PART II

Confronting Shame

1

Shame and the Meaning of Being Human

By its own example as well as by its core message, then, Alcoholics Anonymous teaches that there is a wholeness in limitation. This understanding echoes an ancient tradition of wisdom, which saw being human as being caught in the middle, containing a contradiction. To be human, according to this tradition, means to sustain the tension of always being pulled in two opposite directions: to be more than human and to be less than human.

This vision has haunted many thinkers. Two very different philosophers, whose thoughts span centuries, can clarify its meaning for us; for their insights anticipate two descriptions of alcoholic experience that may be heard detailed at virtually any meeting of Alcoholics Anonymous. Their vision posits an image: man, located on the scale of reality between "beast" and "angel," contains within himself *both* "beast" *and* "angel." To be human, then, is to experience from within the contradictory pulls to be both angel and beast, both more and less than merely human. Because of these contradictory pulls, to be human is to live in a tension: because one is pulled to both, one can exclusively attain neither. Yet the tension pinches and strains; and some humans strive to resolve it by becoming only one or the other, beast or angel.

Over three hundred years ago, the French mathematician and mystic Blaise Pascal observed of one such effort: "He who would be an angel becomes a beast."[8] That is, the attempt to be more than human leads to being less than human. Early in the present century, the Spanish-born, Harvard philosopher George Santayana utilized the same image to make its complementary point: "It is necessary to become a beast if one is ever to be a spirit."[9] To attain the heights of human existence, one must also touch its depths.

Together, these understandings and their point—as both angel and beast, one cannot be only either—embrace the core perception and process of Alcoholics Anonymous. In the A.A. understanding that can be heard, paraphrased, at any A.A. meeting, the alcoholic drank in the attempt or claim to be one or the other, angel or beast; the essence of sobriety resides in the acceptance that one is both—that because one can be only both, the effort to be only one or the other dooms one to insatiable frustration.

This vision of the human as both angel and beast thus captures well the descriptions of drinking experience heard within Alcoholics Anonymous—the vivid portrayal of the heights and the depths reached for and even attained, only to have their opposites relentlessly and inevitably recur. This understanding of the meaning of being human emphasizes the essential incongruity—the inherent conflict, contradiction, antinomy—at the very core of the human condition. Much literature explores this theme of inherent incongruity, sensitively delineating the painful paradox of human aspiration conjoined with human finitude, human hope subverted by human limitation.

Yet the paradox need not be only painful. One of its modern students, the anthropologist Ernest Becker in his Pulitzer prize-winning study of *The Denial of Death,* has captured its essence in a striking phrase that not only can further our appreciation of the paradox but that can reveal the humor that lies on the other side of its pain. And that insight into humor can deepen our understanding of how Alcoholics Anonymous heals shame. In Becker's vivid and memorable image, to be human is to be "a god who shits."[10]

The humor of being human

Humor, in a definition that reflects itself, "arises from the perception of the juxtaposition of incongruity." We find funny the placing together of things that do not belong together: the portly, top-hatted, distinguishedly pompous gentleman slipping on a banana peel, for example. Humor and laughter may, of course, be aggressive and even cruel—especially when the other is objectified rather than identified with. But when humor's incongruity is recognized as inherent—a reflection of the essential contradiction of being human with which one identifies—there can be no more healing, whole-ing, experience than the laughter that marks identifying acceptance of that paradoxical incongruity.[11]

Such laughter characterizes meetings of Alcoholics Anonymous, revealing much about A.A.'s healing power. The stories told at these meetings exquisitely demonstrate the essential incongruity of the human condition, the humor inherent in being human.

> I'd sit up all night, just about, watching the late late *late* movies, tears streaming down my face, thinking "Yes, that's how life really is, loveless and tragic"; and I'd toast each sad revelation with another warming swallow of booze. During the breaks I'd go out to the kitchen to get more ice, and passing the hall mirror I'd look soulfully at my image in it—with immense, enormous self-pity, but with no realization at all that the bleary-eyed, puffy, unshaven condition of my face and its booze-stinking breath just might have something to do with my being unloved.

Or:

> When I first came around A.A., someone suggested that I get down on my knees each morning and ask for help to not take a drink that day. Well, I resented that! Me, kneel down and ask for help? No way ... so I didn't come back, for a while. Instead I went back to drinking, my usual pattern, until one morning it came to me. There I was, in my accustomed morning position, kneeling on the cold tile of my bathroom floor with my arms wrapped around the toilet heaving my guts out. The thought crossed my mind that it wasn't the kneeling or the asking for help that bothered me—after all, that's just what I was doing! It was that those A.A.'s wanted me to do it on a warm, carpeted floor with a serene stomach! And if that was what bothered me, maybe they were right and I *was* "sick," and so I decided to give you folks another try.

Such humor and the laughter that greets it are never aimed at others as objects, but at the contradictions within self illumined by the human experience described. A.A. laughter expresses appreciation of the insights into self garnered from the experience of others with whom one identifies. Thus, humor within Alcoholics Anonymous witnesses to A.A. members' acceptance of the paradoxical nature of the human condition—essentially limited but inherently striving for the unlimited. In attempting and claiming to attain transcendence by their use of alcohol, alcoholics come to touch—even to wallow in—the depths of their own finitude.

Recognizing the incongruity between that endeavor and its result frees from both. Such humor is neither veiled aggression nor mere compensation; it rather manifests the central animus of A.A.'s understanding of human nature. The human essence resides in the human condition's conjunction of infinite thirst with essentially limited capacity. Acceptance of this reality comes easily to the alcoholic who understands her alcoholism; the phenomenon of alcoholism replicates the essence of the human condition.[12]

[handwritten note in top margin: Emphasis on control as but not limited to be addicted]

2

Two Corollaries of Shame

[handwritten note: you can do something, but not everything]

Its own example in accepting limitation and the gift of healing humor that its meetings offer are not the only ways in which Alcoholics Anonymous inculcates in its members the acceptance of essential limitation that enables constructive confrontation with shame. A.A.'s insight into the human condition suggests another understanding, one that illumines both its diagnosis and its healing of the alcoholic. As Bill Wilson never tired of reminding, "the alcoholic is an all-or-nothing person."[13] The futility of this effort to deny the essential some-ness of the human experience manifests itself in especially two areas—control and dependence.

In the A.A. understanding, the drinking alcoholic drinks alcohol in an effort to achieve control—*absolute* control—over his feelings and environment; yet his drinking itself is absolutely out of control. Similarly, the drinking alcoholic denies all dependence. She drinks in an attempt to deny dependence upon others, upon anything outside herself; but her dependence upon alcohol itself has become absolute. The alcoholic's problem, then, involves the demand for absolute control and the claim to be absolutely independent. A.A.'s healing attacks this double problem in a two-fold way. First, the alcoholic is confronted with the facts that, so far as alcohol is concerned, he is absolutely out of control and absolutely dependent. Then, when this reality (contained in the very concept "alcoholic") has been accepted by the admission of "powerlessness over alcohol," Alcoholics Anonymous prescribes limited control and limited dependence.

An image, an ancient posture, clarifies the relationship between the human-as-middle and its corollaries of limited control and limited dependence. In the original, privately published version of A.A.'s Twelve Steps, the Seventh Step opened with the phrase: "Humbly on our knees …"[14]

Kneeling, the Pietist posture, is a middle position—half-way between standing upright and lying flat. A.A.'s interpretation of the alcoholic condition may be conceptualized around this image. The alcoholic is one who, in his claim to absolute independence and absolute control over alcohol, insists on trying to stand unaided, only to inevitably fall flat on his face—often literally in the gutter. To the alcoholic lying prone, Alcoholics Anonymous suggests: "Get up on your knees—you can do something, but not everything." Later, in the alcoholic's progress toward sobriety, A.A. often has occasion to temper tendencies to grandiosity with a similar suggestion: "Get down on your knees—you can do something, but not everything." A.A.'s insight into the middleness of the human condition—its limited control and limited dependence—linchpins the fellowship's total approach to the alcoholic, drinking or sober.

The emphasis on control as limited, as neither absolute nor to be abdicated, pervades the A.A. program. "You can do something, but not everything": A.A. members are warned against promising to "never drink again." They learn, rather, "not to take the first drink, one day at a time." They learn to pick up the telephone instead of the bottle. They are encouraged to attend A.A. meetings, which they can do, rather than to avoid all contact with alcohol, which they cannot do. The A.A. sense of limited control is admirably summed up in the famed "Serenity Prayer" that the fellowship originally borrowed from a newspaper obituary: "God grant me the serenity to accept the things I cannot change, the courage to change the things I can, and the wisdom to know the difference."[15]

The "can" and "cannot" of the Serenity Prayer well inculcate the concepts of limited control and limited dependence. They also clarify the depth of the dedication of Alcoholics Anonymous to human freedom. In the A.A. understanding, alcoholism is an obsessive-compulsive malady: the active alcoholic is one who *must* drink, who *cannot* not-drink. Therefore the alcoholic who joins the A.A. fellowship and embraces its program does not thereby surrender her freedom to drink; rather, she gains the freedom to not-drink—no small liberation for one obsessively-compulsively addicted to alcohol. Within Alcoholics Anonymous, indeed, the passage from "mere dryness" to "true sobriety" consists precisely in the change of

perception—perspective—by which the A.A. member mu.
preting his situation as the prohibition, "I cannot drink" to understa..
its deeper reality as the joyous affirmation, "I *can* not-drink."

For the alcoholic, freedom consists in not drinking; and, as any sober
A.A. member will readily testify, there is a world of difference between the
necessary first stage of accepting the limitation "I cannot drink" and
embracing the freedom of the happy new reality "I can not-drink." A.A.'s
success derives in no small part from the fact that it is the only modality
for the healing of alcoholics that contains a philosophy that embraces and
teaches such an understanding of the reality of human freedom.

"Limited control," however, is but one side of the coin of human freedom: its obverse face reveals limited dependence. Here, the philosophy of
Alcoholics Anonymous again subtly challenges a frequent, modern
assumption. Most therapies approach the alcoholic from a point of view
that sees all dependence—but especially the dependence that binds the
alcoholic to his chemical—as humiliating and dehumanizing. They tell the
alcoholic that maturity—becoming fully human—involves overcoming all
such dependencies. Diagnosing alcoholism, virtually all modern therapies
proclaim that the alcoholic's problem is "dependence on alcohol," and
they endeavor to break the alcoholic's dependence.

The larger-wisdomed insight of Alcoholics Anonymous does not exactly
contradict this understanding. Indeed, A.A. agrees with and accepts this
diagnosis that the alcoholic's problem is "dependence on alcohol." But
Alcoholics Anonymous locates the definition's deeper truth by shifting its
implicit emphasis. A.A. interprets the experience of its members as revealing that the alcoholic's problem is not "*dependence* on alcohol," but
"dependence on *alcohol*." To be human, to be essentially limited, Alcoholics Anonymous insists, *is* to be essentially dependent. The alcoholic's
choice—the *human* choice—lies not between dependence and independence, but between that upon which one will acknowledge dependence: a
less than human substance such as alcohol within oneself, or a more than
individual reality that remains essentially outside—beyond—the self.

3

The Qualities of Shame

We seem, perhaps, to have come a long way, a far distance, from our stated topic of shame and guilt. Yet have we? Shame, recall, arises from the feeling of failure, from the sense of falling short. But, in the understanding of the human condition mediated by Alcoholics Anonymous, to be human *is* to fall short. Any healing of shame, then, must confront the inevitability of falling short that the alcoholic—or any other "all-or-nothing person"—seeks to avoid or to deny by such measures as the use of alcohol.

How is this to be done? The confrontation with shame, the acceptance of self as essentially limited, involves two stages: (1) recognizing shame for what it is, and especially its distinction from guilt; (2) finding and applying the mode of healing that enables one to live constructively with one's own essential limitation and therefore with that positive shame without which one becomes "shameless." We turn then, first, to the qualities that characterize shame: avenues that open to touching shame and therefore to embracing one's own essential limitation.

Three characteristics of shame—or better, of its occasion—both aid in distinguishing shame from guilt and illumine the nature of the essential limitation that lies at the core of being human. Guilt, recall, arises from the violation of some restraining boundary: it characteristically has to do with moral transgression, results from a voluntary act, and tends to be proportionate to the gravity of the offense committed. Shame, in contrast, can be recognized because it may be evoked by a non-moral lapse, may arise for an involuntary act, and tends to be magnified by the very triviality of its stimulus.

The non-moral

Shame may arise from either a moral or a non-moral lapse. For some, the possibility of non-moral shame provides the key to understanding its differentiation from guilt. Two cases of non-moral shame are especially relevant in the present context: failure in love and the failure of sickness.

Perhaps the most common source of non-moral shame is disappointment or frustration, and specifically disappointment in love. One who seeks to win another's love, and fails, suffers not the guilt of moral transgression but the constricted hollowness of felt inadequacy. Experiences of defeat, disappointment, frustration, or failure evoke shame. Guilt, as transgression, always involves aggression: one feels guilty about the aggression. Shame, although it may involve an aspect of aggression, arises over the attempt's failure rather than over the attempt itself.[16]

Both the "disease-concept of alcoholism" and A.A.'s emphasis on alcoholism as "malady" serve to bring the alcoholic's drinking under the heading of shame.[17] To be ill is not to transgress, but to fall short. One large contribution of Alcoholics Anonymous has been to remove alcoholism from moral categories. This removal, of course, is more easily claimed than achieved; but distinguishing between guilt and shame can help further that achievement.

The alcoholic who knows from experience that she should not drink alcohol but who obsessively-compulsively does drink it will of course and inevitably feel "bad." If she knows only the category of guilt, she cannot help but judge her drinking to be somehow a moral transgression. Learning the disease concept enables transcending guilt by inviting confrontation with shame. A.A.'s contribution here is to distinguish clearly between the guilty feeling of wickedness and the shamed sense of worthlessness. The experience of Alcoholics Anonymous teaches that the alcoholic's key problem is not that he is wicked, but that he feels worthless. A.A.'s healing, then, touches most deeply not guilt but shame.

The involuntary

The concept of disease and the experience of many diversely sick people who are ashamed of their illnesses also clarify the second characteristic of occasions of specifically shame—their involuntariness. That shame arises involuntarily, from the failure of choice, should be clear from its very concept as outlined near the beginning of this piece. Guilt implies choice; haggling over guilt often focuses upon the question of how free was the choice, but the fact of choice is assumed. Shame, on the other hand, occurs over a falling short, a *missing* of the mark, a *failure* of powers.[d]

> [d]A "missing of the mark": those familiar with ancient languages or theological thought may recognize the concept of *hamartia*—an ancient term for "sin."

Involuntariness is a necessary concomitant of shame's focus upon the deficiency of self. The core of the pain in shame arises from the insufficiency of will. An example may clarify. One seduced into adultery might feel both guilt and shame: guilt over the violation of the marriage promise; shame at falling short of the marriage ideal. The man who finds himself sexually impotent with a woman he loves will feel predominantly shame: the question of morality does not enter, and—at least in his conscious mind—his sexual disability is anything but voluntary.

When an alcoholic says "Why?": "Why do I drink (or do x)—I know I don't want to!" someone imbued with the philosophy of Alcoholics Anonymous knows better than to try to probe and to prove that he really did want to. The A.A. answer, accepting involuntariness, is simple. "You didn't want to, but you did. You did because you are an alcoholic. That is what an alcoholic is: one who drinks when he doesn't want to. The answer to 'Why' lies not in your will or in some unconscious drive, but in the fact that you are an alcoholic ... the simple fact that you are 'all too human.'"

Experiences of shame are valuable because, by their involuntariness, they teach about the limitation of human will. The alcoholic cannot will to not-drink any more than the insomniac can will to fall asleep. The example is exact; for, in both cases, one can will the means, but any attempt directly to will the end proves self-defeating. There are, it seems, two distinct kinds of "will," two different realms in which human will operates. In some matters, will chooses to move in a certain direction; in others, will chooses to possess a particular object. Problems arise when we attempt to apply the will of the second realm—the utilitarian will that chooses objects—to those portions of life that, because they are directions or orientations, wilt or even vanish under such coercion.

Let me try to clarify by suggesting a few other examples, probably familiar to anyone, of this distinction: I can will knowledge, but not wisdom; submission, but not humility; self-assertion, but not courage; congratulations, but not admiration; religiosity, but not faith; reading, but not understanding; physical nearness, but not emotional closeness; dryness, but not sobriety.[e]

> [e]Several of these examples, and the ideas in this and the following paragraph, have been suggested and are treated at greater depth in two essays by Leslie H. Farber: "Thinking About Will" and "Will and Anxiety," in *Lying, Despair, Jealousy, Envy, Sex, Suicide, Drugs, and the Good Life* (New York: Basic Books 1976), pp. 3-34.

Because shame often arises from the failure of the effort to will what cannot be willed, experiences of shame contain an important lesson, and not only for the alcoholic. To know shame is to realize that certain things—the realm of orientation and direction, as in the examples above—fall beyond the scope of the utilitarian will that chooses objects. This realization is important because a major source of anxiety is the effort to will what cannot be willed. The addict seeks chemical relief from such anxiety because drugs—for example, alcohol—offer the illusion of healing this split between the will and its impossible goal. Addiction, indeed, *is* the effort to will what cannot be willed.

The recovering alcoholic or addict knows that such chemical pacification is "illusion," but its remembered attractiveness can haunt one pinched by the pain of anxiety. Insofar, then, as will and its failure enter into the alcoholic's problem, experiences of shame offer a potent reminder of the essential limitation of will with which the alcoholic—like any human—must learn to live.

The trivial

The third and final characteristic of shame to be examined is the apparent disproportion that renders shame literally so monstrous an experience. Usually, the depth and extent of guilt correlate with the gravity of the offense: the more serious the transgression, the greater the guilt. Shame, on the contrary, tends to be triggered by the most trivial of stimuli, by some seemingly small and even picayune detail. Such details, precisely as trivial, reveal most unmistakably the deficiency of self as self rather than as violator of some abstract code. The employee who embezzled ten thousand dollars, when he comes to doing his Eighth and Ninth—amends—Steps, tends to feel predominantly guilt. The person who has cadged quarters off his co-workers' desks, who has habitually ignored the office coffee-pot's plea for coin contributions, will feel more shame than guilt. If a sensitive therapist can tap that shame, can touch that triviality, she will more acutely and thoroughly help one contemplating A.A.'s Eighth and Ninth Steps to confront himself as he is. The trivial invites examining "What kind of person am I to have done that?" The more trivial the "that," the more readily the emphasis moves to "person."[18]

The disproportion that tends to inhere in shame—its tendency to be greater according as its stimulus is smaller—reveals another intriguing facet of shame that renders it especially appropriate for the kind of healing made available by Alcoholics Anonymous. In one sense, albeit not technically, shame is addictive. The disproportion inherent in it serves to magnify shame, for one becomes ashamed at the very inappropriateness of one's reaction, and therefore ashamed of shame itself. Perhaps because of this insatiable quality in shame over the trivial, it is upon the disproportion inherent in experiences of shame that the program of Alcoholics Anonymous fastens in turning shame to constructive use.

Alcoholics Anonymous locates the "root of [the alcoholic's] troubles" in the selfishness of "self-centeredness"—in pride.[19] The drinking alcoholic tends to deem himself exceptional, different, special; and this tendency does not suddenly cease in early sobriety. Thus, one trap for the newly recovering alcoholic, freshly enthusiastic about his dawning recovery, lies in the temptation to judge himself, as he reviews his personal history of alcoholism, especially "wicked." As one observer acutely noted of both drinking and sober alcoholics: "The alcoholic's problem is not that he feels, 'I am a worm,' nor even that he feels, 'I am very special.' The main obstacle to recovery is that the alcoholic is convinced that 'I am a very special worm.'" Admittedly, the telling of stories at Twelve-Step meetings can on occasion exacerbate this problem by degenerating into "Can you top this?" competitions. Yet as usually and properly used, the telling of stories at such meetings, and especially the program's Fifth Step, offer a healing that skirts the "very special worm" trap.

"Admitted to God, to ourselves, and to another human being, the exact nature of our wrongs." Such confession is, of course, ancient religious practice. Yet within Alcoholics Anonymous as within its parent Oxford Group, this practice ministers to shame more than to guilt. The essential point was already clear in the Oxford Group understanding: "This sharing leads to the discovery that sins we thought were so bad are quite run-of-the-mill. The regard of one's sins as particularly awful is a vicious form of pride that is overcome by sharing."[20] A.A.'s Fifth Step, like its practice of story-telling, serves to inculcate a similar awareness: the alcoholic, essentially limited, is very ordinary. This is why A.A.'s Fifth Step is presented as ending "the old pangs of anxious apartness" and beginning the alcoholic's "emergence from isolation."[21]

"I am a very special worm"

4

Shame, Exposure, Denial, and Hiding

Because of the disproportion inherent in shame, because shame's stimulus is so often trivial and shame itself therefore usually so surprising, experiences of shame are experiences of exposure. Experiences of shame throw a flooding and searching light on what and who we are, painfully uncovering unrecognized aspects of personality. Exposure—*exposure to oneself*—lies at the heart of shame.

The root meaning of the word "shame" implies this process: to uncover, to expose, to wound. Experiences of shame are thus experiences of the exposure of peculiarly sensitive, intimate, vulnerable aspects of the self. The exposure may be to others; but, whether others are involved or not, the significant exposure is always to one's own eyes. An incident described by Somerset Maugham in his study *Of Human Bondage* vividly penetrates to the essence of shame as the exposure to oneself of one's own weakness.[22]

The protagonist in the story, Philip, as a new boy at school, was ragged by his classmates who demanded to see his clubfoot. Despite his almost obsequious desire for friendship, Philip adamantly refused to show his handicap. Finally, one night, a group of boys attacked Philip in his bed, and the school bully twisted his arm until Philip stuck his leg out of the bed to let them see his deformity. The boys then laughed and left. And then,

> Philip … got his teeth in the pillow so that his sobbing should be inaudible. He was not crying for the pain they had caused him, nor for the humiliation he had suffered when they looked at his foot, but with rage

at himself because, unable to stand the torture, he had put out ... .
on his own accord.

Exposure to others of his physical deformity was less painful to Philip
than the exposure to himself of his own weakness.

Alcoholism—indeed, any form of addictive dependency—often arises
from and usually is connected with the effort to conceal such weakness, to
prevent its exposure to oneself. The alcoholic or addict uses his chemical in
order to hide, and especially to hide from himself. The endeavor to hide
reveals that the critical problem underlying such behavior is shame.[23]

Guilt moves to solving problems; shame leads to hiding feelings.
"Wanting to be absolved of guilt is not the addict's problem." Usually, the
addicted person within herself is pleading passionately to be able to feel
guilty. Guilt-oriented therapies, however sophisticated, fail because the
addict or alcoholic cannot "mend his ways" or, by willing it, "grow up."
He must maintain his addiction precisely to conceal his unendurable
shame from himself. Any interference with his addictive dependency
threatens to reveal that shame and therefore becomes "a primary survival
threat." In any case in which the avoidance of pain—the existential pain of
shame—plays a basic part in the organization and maintenance of the psy-
chopathology, effective healing must address itself first to the existential
nature of that pain and shame.

This is one reason why effective treatment for the alcoholic involves *caring* rather than *curing*. The approach of Alcoholics Anonymous utilizes the
realization that to induce—or, more exactly, to allow—humiliation can be
an important initial therapeutic goal. The informal format of A.A. meetings, their atmosphere of badinage and humorous confrontation, is well-
designed to achieve this goal.

An often-acted-out image may help to clarify: Any hurting person who
seeks help brings to therapy a tiny, flickering flame of self-esteem. Classic,
guilt-oriented therapies strive to nourish that tiny glimmer, to enlarge self-
esteem. The initial response of Alcoholics Anonymous is different. The
newcomer who leads from self-esteem meets with caring confrontation: he
is offered, for example, a carefully half-filled cup of coffee. Such confrontation of lingering denial invites the hesitant newcomer both to acknowl-

edge the fact of his shakes and to realize that the coffee-server who recognizes the shakes accepts them—and him. The message is less "It's okay" than "It's tough, but I've been there too." Any flicker of self-esteem that signals denial of the felt-worthlessness of shame is gently quashed rather than nourished within A.A. Why? Because A.A. experience testifies that, until that denial is shattered, its own constructive healing cannot be effective. The alcoholic must confront self-as-feared if he is ever to find the reality of self-as-is.

This understanding captures the insight of Dr. Harry Tiebout in his classic psychiatric exploration of the healing dynamic operative in Alcoholics Anonymous.[24] Tiebout distinguished between "compliance," which he saw as worse than useless because it obscured the obsessive-compulsive nature of alcoholism, and "surrender," which he presented as the key to the process of recovery. Tiebout's "compliance" may be understood as motivated by guilt; "surrender," as enabled by the alcoholic's acceptance of his shame.

Denial, Tiebout realized, could continue despite acknowledgment of—despite even attempts at reparation for—guilt. Guilt may even be a defense against confronting and accepting what is denied, as when the alcoholic accepts responsibility for what he has done when drinking as preferable to admitting that the drinking itself was beyond his control. Real guilt fears punishment and tries to escape it. The shamed person, on the other hand, for example the alcoholic just described, may seek and embrace punishment—even by admitting "guilt"—as a confirmation aiding denial of what is most deeply feared: his own failure of being, his sense of having failed as a human being.

Admitting guilt (but not shame) a cover up

PART III

The Healing of Shame

1

Needing Others

In order to get beyond this hiding, in order to transcend this denial, in order to succeed as a human being, any human being needs others. Despite the far too common misunderstanding that has confused shame with embarrassment, "others" are not the problem in shame; they are its solution.

Because of their essential limitation, human beings have needs. The denial of essential limitation usually manifests itself not directly, but in the denial of need. The alcoholic's denial of need is twofold: his denial of his need for alcohol blends into and intertwines with his denial of his need for others. Early in the process of alcoholism, the alcoholic denies that it is his unmet because insatiable need for others that leads him to seek comfort or excitement in alcohol. "A few drinks" become more important than the people at a party, for example, as alcohol becomes a surer source of satisfaction than human interaction. Later in the process, after a few failures of "I can stop whenever I want to" (denial of the need for alcohol) the denial becomes again of the need for others: "Just leave me alone—I can lick this thing by myself."

Alcoholics Anonymous breaks through these twin denials of need. As fellowship, A.A. invites the alcoholic to discover her own need for others by being the one place where the alcoholic herself is needed, and needed precisely and only *as* alcoholic. This leads to self-identification as "alcoholic," and thus to admission of the need for alcohol. As program, A.A. builds on the admission of the need for alcohol—"I am an alcoholic"—ever deepening awareness of one's need for others. The Twelve Steps of the program of Alcoholics Anonymous begin with the word "We," and A.A. ever emphasizes that it is "fellowship" as well as "program." Thus, the vicious circle of denial of need—for alcohol and for others—is broken and replaced by a twofold, mutually enhancing admission of need.

The "need for others" is, of course, the most famous facet of Alcoholics Anonymous. Those outside A.A. often regard it condescendingly, interpreting it away as "the substitution of a social dependence for a drug dependence";[25] or as "accepting the emotional immaturity of alcoholics and supplying a crutch for it."[26]

Yet independent observers have also recognized positive aspects in the acceptance of the human need for others as inculcated by Alcoholics Anonymous. One psychiatrist located the reason for A.A.'s success in this approach, which—as opposed to some mere disease concept of alcoholism—inculcates in the alcoholic and many who would help him the "understanding that human involvement is needed."[27] Alcoholics Anonymous itself, faithful to its Tenth Tradition, remains silent in the midst of this controversy. A.A.—that is, A.A. members—simply performs its chosen task—helping alcoholics get and stay sober. And awarely or not, they do this in part by healing shame.

2

Shame, Objectivity, and Caring

In dealing with shame, other people are not the problem: they are the solution. Both guilt and shame are characterized by "shoulds," but it is the "should" of guilt that comes from outside, from rules made by others. The "should" of shame arises from within, from the nature of the human as essentially limited, yet craving infinity.

Another way of stating this is to observe that guilt is objective; shame, subjective. Because it comes from outside, guilt arises objectively: the line that is crossed, the rule that is broken, has objective existence outside oneself. Shame, in contrast, is a more subjective experience: the goal fallen short of, the self-ideal that quests and claims unlimitedness—these are part of one's own nature, of the be-ing that one "owns." Because of this, shame cannot be healed "objectively."

A funny thing about the modern world: the term "objective" tends to have a good connotation; the term "subjective," to be pejorative. "Objectivity" is a praiseworthy goal: to speak "objectively" is to require credence; calling someone's presentation "objective" is to praise it. The parallel terms "subjectivity," "subjectively," and "subjective" are, on the contrary, putdowns. One hears before them "merely," the implication of flaw and error. We live in a world, indeed, in which "objective" equates with *real*, whereas "subjective" is taken to mean false, unreal, imaginary.

Objectivity is especially desired and valued in the medical—curing—model. We need think no further than the example of the surgeon. Surgeons do not operate on their own family members, on persons with whom they have a caring relationship. Further, even the ordinary patient's body is so prepared and draped for surgery that his personhood and individuality are concealed insofar as possible. Everything about the aura, rit-

35

ual, and procedures of the operating theater is designed to enable the surgeon to perform her skill upon a body rather than upon a person.

In dealing with things as do the physical sciences, or in applying the curing model to human bodies as does medical science, "objectivity" is an obvious virtue. Objects are "out there": how the perceiver relates to them does not make a difference to them. As for the perceiver, "objectivity" enhances her observations of and actions upon objects.[28]

But applied to human beings *as* human beings, as persons who are also subjects, the subject-object model with its demand for "objectivity" dooms to failure. Thinking in terms of subject-object renders others "they"—necessarily apart from and over-against the self. Such a result, indeed such an effort, inevitably distorts: human phenomena are never merely objects. In dealing with human phenomena, that is to say, the flaw of "mereness" inheres in objectivity rather than in subjectivity.

Accepting persons as ends-in-themselves, the Kantian imperative, is impossible in a Cartesian world of subject-object relationships. Such acceptance of persons as persons becomes possible only in a world-view that transcends the subject-object dichotomy—a world in which human relationships can be reciprocal and mutual because the subjectivity, the personhood, of each individual is accepted as first truth. Alcoholics Anonymous is not the only entity to postulate such a vision, such a reality, such a model of caring. But it is specifically the A.A. world-view that concerns us here, and therefore it is the understanding of human relationships that is witnessed to by the experience of Alcoholics Anonymous that we shall examine in this exploration of the healing of shame.

3

Complementarity and the Mutualities that Heal Shame

Within Alcoholics Anonymous, human relationships are characterized by complementarity and mutuality. *Complementarity* means that individuals *fit into* each other, thus enhancing each other rather than merely "bumping into" and so chipping away at, diminishing, self and others. In such relationships, each is to each other according to the needs of both. *Mutuality* underlines this back-and-forth-ness: the two-way, reciprocal nature of relationships that are truly human.

Such relationships furnish the invitation and the opportunity to grow and to expand; they are, indeed, the only way to grow as human. As one profound student of the phenomenon of shame has observed:

> The ability to enter into relations of intimacy and mutuality opens the way to experiences in which the self expands beyond its own limitations in depth of feeling, understanding, and insight. One's own identity may be not weakened, but strengthened by the meaning one has for others ... and by respect for these other persons as distinct individuals.
>
> This experience involves the risk of trusting oneself to other persons instead of regarding them in object, status, or audience relations. It also means not allowing disappointment in response from another person to lead to a denial of the expectation and possibility of love.... A person who is unable to love cannot reveal himself.[29]

Members of Alcoholics Anonymous achieve this ability and experience—this vision of complementary mutuality—by deriving their awareness of their need for others from the fundamental realization that they, as alcoholic, as essentially limited, can be fulfilled, made whole, only by other essentially limited beings who also accept that limitation ... by other alcoholics.

The acceptance of essential limitation is not merely privative, the recognition of a lack. A.A. members find a positive identity in their essential limitation. Within Alcoholics Anonymous, the identification, "I am an alcoholic," is spoken not hesitatingly, in shy embarrassment, but as a joyous affirmation. For within that setting of individuals who accept their own essential limitation, one realizes not only that one needs others, but that one is oneself needed by those others: thus the foundation for mutuality is established.

Making a difference

It is this perception and acceptance of mutuality that enables transcending the "self-centeredness" that members of Alcoholics Anonymous understand to be "the root of our troubles." The mutualities that Alcoholics Anonymous teaches, enables, and lives out are especially three: they involve making a difference, honesty and dependence.

The sense that one is able to make a difference is a deeply basic human need; indeed, Alcoholics Anonymous very unintentionally founded its fellowship upon this vital need. For five months after A.A.'s chronologically first co-founder stopped drinking, he found no one willing to accept his help. Then, alone in "the hick-town" of Akron, Ohio, in May 1935, William Griffith Wilson, the sophisticated New Yorker, discovered that he *needed* another alcoholic if he himself was to stay sober, and so he began the series of telephone calls that led to his first meeting with Doctor Robert Holbrook Smith, not for the purpose of helping Doctor Bob, but for what Bob, as another alcoholic, could give him. Perhaps an even more significant moment occurred some days later at the bedside of the alcoholic who was to become "A.A. Number Three." Wilson and Smith told Bill D. that talking with him was the only way they could stay sober. Bill D. believed them, and therefore he listened:

All the other people that had talked to me wanted to help me, ᵕ pride prevented me from listening to them, and caused only resentment on my part, but I felt as if I would be a real stinker if I did not listen to a couple of fellows for a short time, if that would cure them.[30]

Later wise men have shared the same insight. The psychoanalyst R. D. Laing, for example, criticized the classic therapeutic approach as defective precisely because of the model that classic therapists present: "A prototype of the other as giver but not receiver ... tends to generate in self a sense of failure.... Frustration becomes despair when the person begins to question his own capacity to 'mean' anything to anyone."[31] Elsewhere, Laing goes further, suggesting explicitly that the sense of being "not able to make a difference" issues in shame and despair rather than guilt: "the person experiences, not the absence of the presence of the other, but the absence of his own presence as other for the other."[32]

To appreciate the human necessity for a feeling of efficacy, the human need to make a difference, is to touch the depths of the wisdom of Alcoholics Anonymous. Precisely here, A.A. taps one of the few unchanging facets of the essence of the human condition. Ponder, for example, in this context of how A.A. works, this insight (again Laing's) into the nature of the thirst of modern mankind:

Every human being, whether child or adult, seems to require *significance*, that is *place in another person's world.*... It seems to be a universal human desire to wish to occupy a place in the world of at least one other person. Perhaps the greatest solace in religion is in the sense that one lives in the Presence of an Other.[33]

And, one might add, in "the Presence of an Other to whom what one does makes a difference."

Mutuality means making a difference not by "giving and getting" but by giving *by* getting, getting *by* giving. This reciprocal conjunction of the experience of giving and the experience of receiving characterizes not only Alcoholics Anonymous, but all expressions of human love. This reality of love is one deep reason why Alcoholics Anonymous works.

We ourselves want to be needed. We do not only have needs, we are also strongly motivated by *neededness*.... We are restless when we are not needed, because we feel "unfinished," "incomplete," and we can only get completed in and through these relationships. We are motivated to search not only for what we lack and need but also for that for which we are needed, what is wanted from us.[34]

Honesty with self and others

The second mutuality taught by and put into practice within Alcoholics Anonymous involves honesty. A.A. experience teaches that there exists an essential mutuality between honesty with self and honesty with others: both may be present or both may be absent, but neither can exist for any length of time without the other. Most newcomers to Alcoholics Anonymous come to understand the necessary mutuality between honesty with self and with others precisely from their personal experience of the inevitable mutuality of dishonesty with self and others.

> Those who deceive themselves are obliged to deceive others. It is impossible for me to maintain a false picture of myself unless I falsify your picture of yourself and me.[35]

> ... it is a form of self-deception to suppose that one can say one thing and think another.[36]

As with the mutuality of making a difference, of giving and getting, the mutuality involved in honesty and dishonesty with self and others is not a unique discovery of Alcoholics Anonymous. The most profound description of the process underlying this mutuality has been offered by the research psychoanalyst who was called "the poet-philosopher of the current human condition," Dr. Leslie H. Farber. His insight merits quotation at length, for it captures a theme heard often in the personal histories narrated at meetings of Alcoholics Anonymous—and not only at meetings of Alcoholics Anonymous:

> As a child grows gradually aware of the absolute separateness of his being from all others in the world, he discovers that this condition offers both pleasure and terror ... To the extent that he must—or

believes that he must—toy with his own presentation of himself to others to earn the attention and approval he craves … he will experience a
queer, unnamable apprehension…. This uneasy state is both painful
and corrupting.

It is commonly believed that this pain and corruption are consequences
of his low self-esteem and fear of others' indifference and rejection, that
these cause him to project himself falsely. It seems more likely that
once this habit begins to harden, the crucial source of pain is his corruption. In his constant inability or unwillingness to tell the truth
about who he is, he knows himself in his heart to be faking.

Not merely is he ashamed of having and harboring a secret, unlovely,
illegitimate self. The spiritual burden of not appearing as the person he
"is," or not "being" the person he appears to be—the extended and
deliberate confusion of seeming and being—is by and large intolerable
if held in direct view. If the integrity he craves is to be denied him, at
least he will have its illusion. If he cannot publicize his private self …
then he will command his private self to conform to the public one.
This beguiles to a loss of truth; not only "telling" it, but *knowing* it.

There are some things it is impossible both to do and at the same time
to impersonate oneself doing. Speaking truthfully is one of them.[37]

There is, thus, a mutuality between honesty with self and honesty with
others: it is necessary to avoid self-deception if one is to be honest with
others, but at the same time one must be honest with others if one is to
avoid self-deception. The drinking alcoholic, if she glimpses this realization at all, finds in it only the most vicious of circles. One gift of A.A.'s
insight is the revelation that this mutuality can enhance growth rather
than hasten self-destruction. How to live its paradoxical wisdom becomes,
for the sober alcoholic, an essential part of her continuing participation in
Alcoholics Anonymous as both fellowship and program.

Dependence and independence

Both mutualities already examined—making a difference and honesty—flow into the third mutuality inherent in A.A.'s healing: that

between dependence and independence. Here also, A.A.'s insight into the essential connection between personal dependence and personal independence derives from its central focus on the reality of essential limitation as the first truth of the human condition. It is because the human is somehow the juncture of the infinite with the limited—because to be human is to be both angel and beast—that human dependence and human independence must be mutually related, not only between people but within each person.

Mutuality means that each enables and fulfills the other. To speak of a mutuality between human dependence and human independence, then, is to point out not only that both are necessary within human experience, but also that each—dependence and independence—becomes fully human and humanizing only by connection with the other.

As already noted, most therapeutic approaches aim to make the alcoholic independent, viewing personal dependence and personal independence as contradictory rather than enhancing. Their goal of independence is not unrelated to their ideal of objectivity and their hope of curing. Yet, as we saw in our treatment of the A.A. goals of limited control and limited dependence, the alcoholic gains the freedom to not-drink only by acknowledging that his problem is not "*dependence* on alcohol," but "dependence on *alcohol*." The experience of Alcoholics Anonymous suggests that dependence is no more "cured" than is alcoholism: rather, the alcoholic's dependence comes to be healed—to be integrated into her whole personality in a way that enhances her humanity—by the mutuality of caring.

For specific reasons within the history of psychological thought, the study of continuing human dependence has not found a central place in any theory of human development.[38] Not too long ago, this surprising lacuna began to be filled. At least one school of analytic psychiatry achieved success by building on the fundamental insight: "Dependence versus independence is the basic neurotic conflict." According to Donald Winnicott, one leader of this school of thought that has given rise to "personal relationship therapy," for the truly mature person, "dependence and independence do not become conflicting issues, rather they are complementary."[39]

The truly mature person, that is, experiences "ontological security." For the individual whose own being becomes secured in this primary experiential sense, to be related with others is potentially gratifying and fulfilling. The "ontologically insecure person," on the contrary, one who has not come to terms with the complementarity of dependence and independence, is pre-occupied with preserving rather than fulfilling self: he becomes obsessed with the task of preventing himself from losing himself. Such an ontologically insecure person reaches out to others in self-seeking dependency, out of the same needs that drive the alcoholic or addict to seek chemical relief. Ontological insecurity undermines any possibility of true mutuality.[40]

To be not-God, to be both beast and angel, is to be neither "all" nor "nothing": one is rather some-one. The acceptance and affirmation of *some*-ness closes the door to the infantile claim to be "all": "His Majesty the Baby," in the Freudian term of Dr. Harry Tiebout. The embrace and cherishing of *one*-ness invites to the joyous pluralism of complementarity that is the essential dynamic of Alcoholics Anonymous: the shared honesty of mutual vulnerability openly acknowledged.

Dependence and independence, then, are mutually related. Independence is enriched by dependence just as our waking hours can be fruitful only if we obtain adequate sleep. Likewise, constructive dependence requires independence just as healthy sleep requires adequate waking exercise. The very rhythms of human life reflect the mutuality inherent in human nature. In a sense one "charges batteries" by dependence, thus enabling independent operation. The reverse of the analogy proves equally true: being dependent without exercising independence is like over-charging a battery rarely used—destructive of both the self and the source.

Alcoholics Anonymous, both in its suggestion of a "Higher Power" and in the way its meetings work, invites and enables the living out of this mutuality between human dependence and personal independence. The First Step of the A.A. program establishes the foundation for this understanding: only by acknowledging continuing dependence upon alcohol does the A.A. member achieve the continuing independence of freedom from addiction to alcohol.

PART IV

Conclusion

1

Being "Both":
The Nature of Freedom

Any true healing of shame will accept the necessary mutualities that flow from the essential limitation of the human condition. It will recognize that "others"—other individuals aware of their own essential limitation—play a twofold role in this healing: (1) their example facilitates the acceptance of one's own limitation; (2) their presence enables a degree of transcendence of limitation, for they invite living the mutualities of making a difference, honesty, and dependence-independence.

Shame contains a "not"—the "not" imposed by essential limitation. That "not" is to be neither severed nor undone: it is lodged in the very essence of our human be-ing. To be honestly human is to be aware that one falls short—to accept that the ability to be is also the ability to be not. Thus, to be human *is* to experience shame—to feel "bad" about the not-ness lodged in one's essence. Why this feeling-bad of shame? Because of the anomalous nature of the human as beast-angel, as essentially limited yet craving unlimitedness. The anomaly is inherent, for to be human is to be "both/and" rather than "either-or." Confronted with the task of being human, one must live *both* its polarities: one cannot be only either. The shame of "feeling to blame" arises from the necessary imperfection of such both-ness: inevitably one falls short of being either beast or angel—neither can be total so long as both are actual.

Within Alcoholics Anonymous, within any group based on the shared honesty of mutual vulnerability openly acknowledged, the individual in the process of recovering her humanity learns that there exists a necessary connection between being limited and being real. The practice of mutual-

47

ity—and it does take "practice"—inculcates the truths that to be real is to be limited, and that to be limited is to be real.

This necessary fact of the human condition is perhaps clearest in the matter of the alcoholic's "freedom" in relation to alcohol. The recovering alcoholic learns first in Alcoholics Anonymous that his freedom, although real, is limited—and that his freedom, although limited, is real. Free to drink, the alcoholic is not free to not drink. To attain the freedom to not drink, the alcoholic accepts limitation of his freedom to drink. But this realization, important as it is, does not suffice for true, joyous sobriety. The alcoholic in recovery must come to see, however hazily, that this acceptance is not a concession. The word "although," that is to say, must be replaced by the affirmation "because": *because* real, freedom is limited; *because* limited, freedom is real.

The ongoing experience of recovery continually reminds the alcoholic how the apparently unlimited freedom to drink inevitably leads to increasing bondage and ever greater losses of freedom (to work, to love and to be loved, to live). The same experience of recovery also progressively reveals, on the other hand, how the limited freedom to not drink brings in its wake ever increasing freedoms. The recovering alcoholic within Alcoholics Anonymous thus learns a profound truth: with freedom as with any other human phenomenon, to be real is to be limited, for limitation *proves* reality. This understanding enables joyous acceptance of the human condition as well as true recovery from alcoholic addiction. It enables these "both" because, at depth, that acceptance and that recovery are one and the same.

In some almost incomprehensible way, the words *sobriety, serenity,* and, yes, *sanctity* name the same reality.

2

Pluralism, Tolerance, Complementarity, and Love

This is the profound lesson of Alcoholics Anonymous: truly human living begins with the creative acceptance of the reality of essential human limitation—with the embrace of the not-ness, the "shame," that inheres at the core of human be-ing. Two final concepts carry that insight to its conclusion as that is lived out in groups rooted in the shared honesty of mutual vulnerability openly acknowledged: *pluralism* and *complementarity*.

Pluralism means accepting that, among those essentially limited, there can be no *one* way of being that is perfect or "best." "Easy Does It," cautions A.A.: "Live and Let Live."

Complementarity suggests that imperfect beings can aid in completing or fulfilling each other. The "experience, strength, and hope" of each alcoholic enhances the experience, strength, and hope of every other alcoholic within A.A.

Alcoholics Anonymous enables—indeed thrives on—pluralistic complementarity because each member not only accepts limitation but finds in that very limitation ("I am an alcoholic") the basis for relating to others within their fellowship. Because they relate to each other so consciously from shared weakness (their alcoholism), A.A. members give and get without threat: alike in weakness, they find in their differences only strength. Most other human associations are formed on the basis of some strength, some positive quality by which one contributes to the group. Members of Alcoholics Anonymous belong to their fellowship because of their weakness, something they cannot do—imbibe alcohol in a way their culture deems normal.

Alcoholics Anonymous arrived at its acceptance of pluralism honestly. The insight, and its implications, were at first uncongenial to a fellowship whose members were characterized by obsessive-compulsive behavior—alcoholics who, as co-founder Bill Wilson never tired of reminding, tended to be "all-or-nothing people." Yet Alcoholics Anonymous, largely through Bill Wilson, learned the lesson of pluralistic tolerance from early on:

> In the early days of A.A. I spent a lot of time trying to get people to agree with me, to practice A.A. principles as I did, and so forth. For so long as I did this ... A.A. grew very slowly.[41]
>
> A.A. works for people with differing views—that is good.[42]
>
> Honesty gets us sober but tolerance keeps us sober.[43]

Very early in A.A. history, indeed, Wilson intuited and skillfully inculcated the unshakeable basis for the fellowship's tolerance of even apparent perversity as well as of every diversity:

> The way our "worthy" alcoholics have sometimes tried to judge the "less worthy" is, as we look back on it, rather comical. Imagine, if you can, one alcoholic judging another![44]

Tolerance flows naturally from A.A.'s central focus on human essential limitation. Because human beings are essentially limited, any individual's possession of truth must be limited, if it is real. In fostering such tolerance, Alcoholics Anonymous teaches not only an openness to pluralism that accepts difference, but the sense of complementarity that welcomes and values diversity: "tolerance keeps us sober." And without differences, after all, there could be no tolerance.

Because of the essential limitation of human existence, because of the mixed nature of the human condition as not-God, as beast-angel, as essentially limited yet craving "more," each human being is incomplete. Because of this incompleteness, each needs others. Because of this essential incompleteness, indeed, each person most clearly discovers and reveals his own nature by the particular ways in which he needs other essentially limited human beings.

Because any "other" is also essentially incomplete, any constructive human relationship is characterized by complementarity—the sense that each fulfills the other. Complementarity, because it is founded on the essential limitation of both, involves acceptance by each of the other as another who is also person, and therefore as concrete, unique, different, potentially enriching individual. This awareness of complementarity opens to the mutual sense of mutual fulfillment. The sense of complementarity consists in the realization that the existence of both is affirmed by each other, that the differences of each enrich rather than threaten the other.

This understanding reflects the model of love hymned throughout the ages by poets and philosophers: biological heterosexuality, the complementarity of male and female. Most obviously in this prototype, love—the mutuality of giving and receiving that enhances and fulfills—flourishes because of difference rather than despite it. Alcoholics Anonymous teaches love because love itself derives from the acceptance of essential human limitation. The denial of essential limitation renders love impossible, for denying limitation and therefore rejecting complementarity leads to demanding in "love" only likeness—a demand that results either in narcissism or in the destructive attempt to impose likeness, and neither of these can be love. The pluralistic insight, the kind of tolerance that derives from the acceptance of essential limitation, on the other hand, finds difference enriching rather than threatening: it thus opens to the love that flourishes not despite difference, but because of it.

Recognizing, admitting, and accepting essential limitation can be terrifying. Consciousness of essential limitation can raise the defenses that wall off others and therefore preclude love. But it need not, as the experience of Alcoholics Anonymous testifies. Members of Alcoholics Anonymous seem not only to grasp but to improve upon Goethe's maxim: "Against the superiority [difference] of another, there is no remedy but love.[45]

Enlarging the possibilities of mutuality—of pluralism and complementarity—requires risk. Expanding the scope of mutual love depends upon risking exposure: the honesty that reveals essential limitation and thus admits need must confront shame. The program and fellowship of Alcoholics Anonymous enable such risk and confrontation by inculcating the qualities of hope and trust that permit truly free choice. Accepting contingency (not-God-ness) equips one to survive and even to flourish in a world of possibility. Such acceptance cures addiction, in the sense that it reveals addiction's inherent untruth.

> Whenever the desire for emotional security becomes primary over all else, for whatever reason, addiction sets in.... Because he is so vulnerable, what the addict is ideally striving for is perfect invulnerability. He only gives himself in exchange for the promise of safety.[46]

But there is no absolute safety, not for the alcoholic, not for the addict, not for any human being. For the human condition admits of neither perfection nor invulnerability. The "experience, strength, and hope" of the members of Alcoholics Anonymous suggest that it is precisely the crack of imperfection, the admission of vulnerability, that reveal—un-veil—the reality of human *be*-ing. And if this be true for alcoholics, perhaps all of us might glimpse its truth for us in a brief meditation:

> Honesty involves exposure: the exposure of self-as-feared that leads to the discovery of self-as-is. Both of these selves are essentially vulnerable: to be is to be able to hurt and to be hurt. But something tells us that we should not hurt: that we should neither hurt others nor hurt within ourselves. Yet we do—both hurt and hurt, both cause and feel pain.

> When we cause pain, we experience guilt; when we feel pain, we suffer shame. The pain, the hurt, the guilt of the first is overt: it exists outside of us, "objectively." The pain, the hurt, the shame of the second is hidden: it gnaws within, it is "subjective." Neither can be healed without confronting the other. A bridge is needed—a connection between the hurt that we cause and the hurt that we are.

> That bridge cannot be built alone. The honesty that is its foundation must be shared. A bridge cannot have only one end. Without sharing, there can be no bridge. But a bridge needs a span as well as foundations. This bridge's span is vulnerability—the capacity to be wounded, the ability to know hurt. "I need" because "I hurt"—if deepest need is

honest. What I need is another's hurt, another's need. Such a need on my part would be "sick"—if the other had not the same need of me, of my hurt and my need. Because we share hurt, we can share healing. Because we know need, we can heal each other.

Our mutual healing will be not the healing of curing, but the healing of caring. To heal is to make whole. Curing makes whole from the outside: it is good healing, but it cannot touch my deepest need, my deepest hurt—my shame, the dread of myself that I harbor within. Caring makes whole from within: it reconciles me to myself-as-I-am—not-God, beast-angel, human. Caring enables me to touch the joy of living that is the other side of my shame, of my not-God-ness, of my humanity.

But I can care, can become whole, only if you care enough—need enough—to share your shame with me.

Could the same be true for you?

About the Author

Ernest Kurtz, who completed his Ph.D. in the History of American Civilization at Harvard University in 1978, was the first researcher to be granted full access to the archives of Alcoholics Anonymous. The book that resulted, *Not-God: A History of Alcoholics Anonymous* (1979), published forty years after the publication of the A.A. Big Book, is still the classic work on the subject. His book on the spiritual life—Ernest Kurtz and Katherine Ketcham, *The Spirituality of Imperfection: Modern Wisdom from Classic Stories* (1992)—is equally well known, and has also been an enduring best seller through the years since it appeared.

He has also contributed numerous articles to scholarly journals on the topic of alcoholism and its treatment, and on the spiritual component of the A.A. approach. A recent selection of some of his articles and essays can be found in Ernest Kurtz, *The Collected Ernie Kurtz* (Wheeling, West Virginia: Bishop of Books, 1999).

Notes

1. [William Griffith Wilson], "The Fellowship of Alcoholics Anonymous," in *Alcohol, Science and Society* (New Haven CT: Yale University Press, 1945), p. 472.

2. Often, the kind of fellowships described here are referred to as "Self-Help Groups." As students of these groups are increasingly recognizing, that term is a misnomer: fellowships such as Alcoholics Anonymous are far more accurately named and understood as "Mutual-Aid Groups." Some reasons for this will be made clear in the concluding part of this presentation.

3. *Cf.* Helen Merrell Lynd, *On Shame and the Search for Identity* (New York: Harcourt, Brace, & World, 1958), pp. 35-36.

4. *Cf.* Lynd, pp. 24-26.

5. *Cf.* William Barrett, *Irrational Man* (New York: Doubleday, 1956), pp. 225-227; on the root, *angh-, cf. The American Heritage Dictionary of Indo-European Roots*, rev. and ed. by Calvert Watkins (Boston: Houghton Mifflin, 1985), p. 2.

6. Letters in which Wilson used the phrases "kindergarten of the spirit" or "spiritual kindergarten" include (all from New York City) to Caryl Chessman, 3 May 1954; to Dr. Tom P., 4 April 1955; to Walter B., 1 July 1958; to Father K., 28 July 1958; to Betty L., 8 December 1967.

7. *Alcoholics Anonymous*, 4th ed. (New York: Alcoholics Anonymous World Services, 2001), pp. 58-60.

8. As quoted by Lucien Goldmann, *The Hidden God* (New York: Humanities Press, 1964), p. 188.

9. As quoted by Morton and Lucia White, *The Intellectual Versus the City* (New York: Mentor, 1964), p. 188.

10. Ernest Becker, *The Denial of Death* (New York: Free Press, 1973), p. 58.

11. *Cf.* Lynd, pp. 94-96, 145-147.

12. On alcoholism as a metaphor for the human condition, *cf.* Ernest Kurtz, *Not-God: A History of Alcoholics Anonymous*, rev. ed. (Center City, MN: Hazelden, 1991), pp. 200-202.

13. *E.g.* Wilson (New York) to Howard Clinebell, 15 November 1960; to Patricia N., 7 January 1963; to Bob C., 23 June 1964.

14. The original wording of A.A.'s Seventh Step may be found in the "Pre-Publication (Multilith) Copy of the Big Book (1939)": *Alcoholic's [sic] Anonymous* (Newark, NJ: Works Publishing, 1939), p. 26; this version and adaptations of it are now (2007) plentifully available on the internet.

15. For the story of A.A.'s discovery and adoption of "The Serenity Prayer," *cf. Alcoholics Anonymous Comes of Age* (New York: A.A. World Services, Inc., 1957), p. 196; *As Bill Sees It* (New York: A.A. World Services, Inc., 1967), p. 108.

16. *Cf.* Helen Block Lewis, Shame and Guilt in Neurosis (New York: International Universities Press, 1971), pp. 81, 84.

17. On "the disease-concept of alcoholism," *cf.* E. M. Jellinek, *The Disease Concept of Alcoholism* (New Haven: College and University Press, 1960; Mark Keller, "The Disease Concept of Alcoholism Revisited," *Journal of Studies on Alcohol* 37 (1976): 1674-1717. *Cf.* also Ernest Kurtz, *Not-God: A History of Alcoholics Anonymous*, rev. ed. (Center City, MN: Hazelden, 1991) pp. 22-23 on A.A.'s use of the term *malady* and Part Two on the "disease-metaphor of alcoholism."

18. *Cf.* Lynd, *On Shame*, pp. 40, 64, 235.

19. *Alcoholics Anonymous*, p. 62.

20. H. J. Almond, "Moral Re-Armament: The Oxford Group" (unpublished Master's thesis, Yale University, 1947), p. 12. [A copy of this thesis, with no further identification, was made available to me by a member of Moral Re-Armament during my own dissertation research that became the book, *Not-God: A History of Alcoholics Anonymous*.]

21. *Twelve Steps and Twelve Traditions* (New York: A.A World Services, 1978), pp. 57, 62; note that this is according to the "Sixteenth Printing, February

1978"; the pagination of this book differs in different printings; earlier than 1978, for example, these quotations appeared on pp. 59 and 63.

22. On the root of *shame, cf.* Joseph T. Shipley, *The Origins of English Words* (Baltimore: Johns Hopkins, 1984), p. 363; also Lynd, *On Shame*, pp. 27-32; the excerpt from Maugham appears on pp. 29-30.

23. For a deeper exploration of this idea, *cf.* David G. Edwards, "Shame and Pain and 'Shut up or I'll Really Give You Something to Cry About,'" *Clinical Social Work Journal* 4 (1976): 3-13; for the quotations in the next paragraph, 7-12.

24. Harry M. Tiebout, "The Act of Surrender in the Therapeutic Process," *Quarterly Journal of Studies on Alcohol* 10 (1959): 48-58; "Surrender Versus Compliance in Therapy," *Quarterly Journal of Studies on Alcohol* 14 (1963): 58-68.

25. Stanton Peele (with Archie Brodsky), *Love and Addiction* (New York: Taplinger, 1975), p. 232.

26. Francis T. Chambers, Jr., "Analysis and Comparison of Three Treatment Measures for Alcoholism: Antabuse, the Alcoholics Anonymous Approach, and Psychotheraphy," *British Journal of Addiction* 50 (1951): 29-41.

27. William Glasser, *The Identity Society* (New York: Harper and Row, 1976), p. 58.

28. I am aware of Heisenberg and the insights others have brought especially to the world of subatomic physics, also of the various vagaries of post-modern imaginings; but as stated here, the point is valid for ordinary people dealing with ordinary realities in ordinary daily life.

29. Lynd, *On Shame*, pp. 159-160.

30. *Alcoholics Anonymous*, 3rd ed. (1976), p. 185.

31. R. D. Laing, *Self and Others* (Baltimore: Pelican, 1971), pp. 84-85.

32. *Ibid.*, p. 138.

33. *Ibid.*, p. 136.

34. Andras Angyal, quoted by Milton Mayeroff, *On Caring* (New York: Harper and Row, 1971), frontispiece.

35. Laing, *Self and Others*, p. 143.

36. R. D. Laing, *The Divided Self* (Baltimore: Penguin, 1965), p. 18.

37. Leslie H. Farber, *Lying, Despair, Jealousy, Envy, Sex, Suicide, Drugs and the Good Life* (New York: Basic Books, 1976), pp. 196-198.

38. A brief summary of this point may be found in Willard Gaylin, "In the Beginning," in Gaylin *et al., Doing Good: The Limits of Benevolence* (New York: Pantheon, 1978), pp. 12 ff. Readers will also find helpful on this and related topics Philip Cushman, *Constructing the Self, Constructing America: A Cultural History of Psychotherapy* (Boston: Addison-Wesley, 1995).

39. This line of thought is best summarized in Harry Guntrip, *Psychoanalytic Theory, Therapy, and the Self* (New York: Basic Books, 1971), *cf.* especially, and for the quotations here, pp. 115, 118, 126, 190.

40. The dangers inherent in the alcoholic's craving for inappropriate dependence were a constant theme of A.A. co-founder Bill W.; *cf.* Kurtz, *Not-God*, pp. 210 ff. and the sources cited there.

41. Wilson (New York) to May M., 24 August 1964.

42. Wilson (New York) to John G., 9 October 1967.

43. [William G. Wilson], "The Fellowship of Alcoholics Anonymous," in *Alcohol, Science and Society* (New Haven: Yale University Press, 1945), p. 472.

44. [Wilson], "Who is a Member of Alcoholics Anonymous—by Bill," *The A.A. Grapevine* 3:3, August 1946, 3.

45. *Gegen grosse Vorzüge eines andern gibt es kein Rettungsmittel als die Liebe.* Johann Wolfgang von Goethe, *Gedenkausgabe der Werke, Briefe und Gespräche*, ed. Ernst Beutler (Zürich: Artemis, 1949), p. 176; a translation may be found in Johann Wolfgang von Goethe, *Elective Affinities*, tr. Elizabeth Mayer and Louise Bogan (Chicago: Henry Regnery, 1963), p. 191.

46. Peele, *Love and Addiction*, pp. 111, 67.

978-0-595-45492-1
0-595-45492-5